THE → S P E E D → WAY

Poems about NASCAR
and Growing Up with Cars and Racing

David B. Axelrod

TotalRecall Publications, Inc.

TotalRecall Publications, Inc.
1103 Middlecreek
Friendswood, Texas 77546
281-992-3131   281-482-5390 Fax
www.totalrecallpress.com

ISBN: 978-1-59095-408-9
UPC   6-43977-64084-0

Printed in the United States of America with simultaneous printings in Australia, Canada, and United Kingdom.

FIRST EDITION
1   2   3   4   5   6   7   8   9   10

For my father, Samuel R. Axelrod,
the best mechanic I ever met.

OTHER BOOKS BY DAVID B. AXELROD

Stills from a Cinema (1968, 1971)

Starting from Paumanok (1972)

Myths, Dreams and Dances (1974)

A Dream of Feet (1976)

A Meeting with David B. Axelrod
and Gnazino Russo (1979)

The Man Who Fell in Love with a Chicken (1980)

Home Remedies: New and Selected Poems (1982)

The End of the Universe (1987)

White Lies (1988)

Resurrections (1989)

A Perpetual Calendar of Poems (1989)

Love in the Keys (1991, 2001)

The Universal Language (1993)

The Chi of Poetry (1995)

Random Beauty (2001)

Another Way (2005)

The Impossibility of Dreams (2007)

Deciduous Poems (2008)

How to Apologize (2009)

Print books available at www.writersunlimited.org
eBooks available at www.totalrecallpress.com

For appearances and workshops, contact:
David B. Axelrod
1104 Jacaranda Avenue
Daytona Beach, FL 32118
386-492-2409
axelrodthepoet@yahoo.com
www.creativehappiness.org
and www.poetrydoctor.org

ACKNOWLEDGMENTS

"Demolition Derby," *Daytona News-Journal*; "Buggy Racing," *White Lies* (Copyright 1988, La Jolla Poets Press); "Time Trials," *Poets in the Park*; "For His Son Who Totaled the Car Again,*" poetry prize winner, *Oberon Magazine* and also in *Long Island Light: Anthology of Long Island Poetry*; "For Richie," "For His Son Who Totaled the Car Again," "Out of Gas #3" (originally as "Breakdown"), *Deciduous Poems* (Copyright 2008, Ahadada Books); "To the Junkyard," "The Body Shop," *Random Beauty* (Copyright 2001; Amereon House); "All Sales Are Final," *Long Island Sounds, 2010*; "The Politics of Ethanol," *Poems and Poets: Anthology for The Year of Poetry*; "How Granny Learned to Love NASCAR," featured in performance by Suffolk County Poet Laureate Edward Stever; "Autographs," *Valparaiso Poetry Review*; "On My Own," *String Poet*; "A History of Speed," *Long Island Quarterly*; "Milkshakes," in Walt's Corner, *The Long Islander*.

Thanks to the following people, who were instrumental in the writing of this book: Sandy Martin, Dan and Emily Axelrod as invaluable editors; Bruce Moran, my publisher; good friends and fellow poets, Adam Fisher, Joe Cavanuagh, Dan Pels and Fred Booth. Thanks to Walter Mims who taught me more about Granny. Thanks to Joan Epton Maxwell at Living Legends of Auto Racing Museum, for keeping me accurate.

PHOTO CREDITS

Cover photo, Kurt Bush © James Tiller, Photo Editor, *Daytona Beach News-Journal*; Photo of Ray Fox book cover, courtesy of Godwin Kelly, Ray Fox and the Living Legends of Auto Racing Museum; Allison family photo © Allison Racing Team, Inc.; Back cover photo by Sandra Martin; "Danica Patrick," "Tangle up," "Kyle Busch" © Walter G. Arce/Shutterstock.com; "Studebaker," Old-timer Picture Gallery/www.autogallery.org; "Dr. Axelrod in the micro-midget," *The Beverly Times* (Beverly, MA, October 9, 1953); "Go-cart teen" © Johannes Gerhardus Swanepoel/dreamstime.com; "Fuel cans and tires" © Lawrence Weslowski, Jr./dreamstime.com; "Horse vs. Car" © *The Boston Phoenix*; "Dale Earnhardt, Jr. talks to crew chief" © JR 88 Rulcs/www.freeimagefinder.com; "The Fans" © Tom Pennington/Getty Images North America; "Pit Crew" © Valli Hilaire/www.flickr.com; "Greg Biffle's car gets inspected" © www. bigstock.com.

FOREWORD

Here's a great new way to enjoy NASCAR and racing. Reading these short pieces about drivers and racing is a fast track into not just the history and the facts but the feelings we share when we participate in stockcar racing.

Poems like "In the Garages" show a great appreciation of the skill it takes to put together a winning team. "A Dozen Fan Poems," catalogs the many ways those attending the races enjoy the experience.

In the personal section of his book, David Axelrod writes about his childhood and later life experiences. "On My Own," and the longer "Buggy Racing," let us see how personal a connection he has to cars and the sport.

You may not think you are a fan of poetry, but this collection should change your mind. Either way, it will certainly appeal to the NASCAR fan in you and entertain you completely.

Robert Coolidge, Vice President
Living Legends of Auto Racing, Inc.

The Living Legends of Auto Racing, Inc. was founded in 1993 to recognize, honor and promote the pioneers of beach racing and stock car racing. Today, the organization has over 600 members from around the world. The all-volunteer, nonprofit organization hosts a variety of activities throughout the year including its annual charity auction and an awards banquet held during the Daytona 500 race week. Living Legends of Auto Racing Museum is located at the Sunshine Park Mall, 2400 South Ridgewood Avenue (US 1), South Daytona, FL 32119. 386-763-4483. Open Monday through Saturday, 10 a.m. to 5 p.m.. Free.

In 1953, 10-year-old David Axelrod is seated at the wheel of the micro-midget racer his father built. His father, Sam, and brother, Don, are behind him. The hood is from a 1940 or '41 Hudson and the steering mechanism is adapted from a Model T Ford. With its 1.5 hp Briggs & Stratton Engine, this midget did 33 mph.

PREFACE

My father, Sam, owned an auto parts store and was a truly talented mechanic who built and owned stock cars that raced at the old West Peabody Speedway in Massachusetts. We spent Saturday evenings at that track. I spent endless hours making my personal version of wooden Soap Box Derby racers that I dragged miles around to compete against friends.

Well before NASCAR was so popular, we spent every Memorial Day weekend glued to the radio and later the TV to follow the Indy 500. I knew every driver's name and stats and got their autographs when they came to town for a racing demonstration. Bill Vukovich, what a driver… and what a shock to see him die in a crash.

Then, there was Grand Prix racing. By my teens, I could do a pretty good Scottish accent, imitating the Indy-Grand Prix winner, Jim Clark, as my cousin, Josh, did the sound effects for race cars whizzing by while we taped mock, track-side interviews.

But what really made me a fan of racing was my father's fault—or great gift. In 1953, when I was just 10, he built the first "micro-midget" race car in our hometown of Beverly, Massachusetts. To the great annoyance of the neighbors and local police, I raced it all over town. On a straightaway at the Beverly Airport, my father drove his wrecker truck along side me and clocked me going 33 mph — better than the half the speed the first race cars hit when Ransom E. Olds brought his own racer to Ormond Beach, Florida, for the first-ever auto race in 1903.

Who would have thought an auto mechanic's son would become a dedicated poet? But that's what happened, and a later-life moment provided the inspiration for this new book of poems. In a conversation not long before my father passed away (at the age of 89) he confessed to me, "I never understood a word of your poetry!" That set me on a path to write a book of short poems that would appeal to everyone, particularly auto racing fans.

This book is based, in part, on my research of auto racing history, but, trained in the university as I am, I still believe that good writing comes from first-hand experience not just reading a lot of books. That's why I went out to meet and interview the fans, drivers, crews, and spent lots of time at NASCAR events.

I also must admit that I indulged myself and spent way too much money fixing up a 1968 Olds Cutlass 442 convertible with a reworked 451 engine. Who cares if the numbers didn't match? I'd take my foot off the brake at a stop light and get whiplash leaving rubber. I've included my own personal experiences because fast cars, racing, love and friendships are intertwined with my life and family.

I hope these poems make an easy and enjoyable read for you. These poems mean what you think. There are no deep, hidden meanings here, and no, there will be no test at the end of the book! Just enjoy the sights, sounds and emotions at the heart of one of America's most popular sports.

David B. Axelrod

Table of Contents

GROWING UP WITH CARS AND RACING   73

NASCAR AND THE SPEEDWAY

Kyle Busch, Kurt's younger brother, wins the Quaker State 400 race at the Kentucky Speedway in Sparta, KY.

TIME TRIALS

No great clamor — rather,
the steady hum of auxiliary
generators keeping the oil
warm, attached to 48 cars
stretching along the pit row,
awaiting 2 timed laps.
Singly, they start their engines,
growl, then roar out onto the track.
With this burst of energy
an order will be set, from
inside and outside pole spots
to the back of the pack.

It's a week before the race,
a world away from a checkered
finish. First in line is Blue 2,
Brad Keselowski, racing since
he was a kid, who says his goal is,
"win anything and everything."
But for now there's that restrictor
plate to change; the new release
valve; which tires to use and an
infinite list of details before
speeds are measured to within
a thousandth of a second.

The Allison family (left to right): Hut Stricklin (Donnie's Son-in-law), Davey Allison, Bobby Allison, Donnie Allison.

Kenny Allison, Ronald Allison, Donald Allison, Clifford Allison

FATHERS AND SONS

(From Allison to Earnhardt, Foyt to Petty, over 2 dozen families, brothers, sons, grandsons, great grandsons, and yes, daughters, too, have competed in NASCAR races.)

If dad does it, and if he brings you
there, chances are you'll want to do it,
too. So imagine Richard, watching
his dad, Lee, powering sideways
through Daytona's north turn, wheels
digging into sand and shells,
defying the corner's reputation
as "The Junkyard." A son would
have to hold his breath and hope
he'd grow up just like dad,
not to mention, grandson Kyle.

Bobby Allison will be hard to beat
with 84 wins over 22 years.
Then, there's brother Donnie,
who's in the Motorsports Hall
of Fame. Imagine, Bobby lost
two sons, Davey and Clifford,
as they pursued their passion
for the sport. Photos show a love
of family and racing so strong
the next generation will surely win.

But for NASCAR, no one beats
William Clifton France, senior
and Bill, Jr., founders of an empire,
whose entire family now shepherds
NASCAR, the Speedway and the sport.

FOR RICHER OR FOR POORER

At first it was a rich man's sport.
In 1903 or 4, about all a common
man could do was pick dead fish
off the beach before the races.
Vanderbilt brought a beast
of a Mercedes that could do 92.
Later, he'd put $6 million into
paving the Vanderbilt Motor Parkway
to speed him from NYC, 45 miles
out on Long Island. In 1910,
Rockefeller, for all his Standard
Oil, loved watching Barney
Oldfield gassing up his Benz
to hit a record 131. Handsome
young men of daring could
do little without the money
to buy $6,000 worth of tires —
the price of 4 race treads,
even in the Depression. When
he came to town in the '30s,
a guy like Bill France was
the opposite of a fat cat. He didn't
have a dime enough to call
a sponsor and ask for money —
just fiddled with cars, opened
the throttle and let loose,
paving the way for generations
of working stiffs to not just watch
but enter their cars. Take Russ
Truelove, a heartthrob on
the track in the mid '50s, out

there in his souped-up Mercury.
He could run flat out for a $5,000
purse, tearing up the beach, racing
north toward Junkyard Turn,
then south on A1A toward fame
and that small fortune. Fast cars,
at last, were for any good man's
pleasure. "If we were lucky,"
Truelove waxed poetic, "we'd
hear the faint whisper of the surf,"
a siren's call to speed as we
risked it all racing along
the beach. Later, he admitted
a driver couldn't hear a thing
over the roar of the engine.

Dale Earnhardt, Jr., talks to his crew chief Steve Letarte.

DALE EARNHARDT, JR.

1.

It's the 10th anniversary
of his dad's death, 1 lap
from winning the 500.
"That changed the sport,"
says everyone — better belts,
barriers, neck braces, safety
a major factor; an outpouring
of grief that made NASCAR
even more popular. But
what does it do to a son?

2.

At the time trials, he draws
applause for opening it up
to 186.364 — good enough to
win the inside pole. It's not
just a record, it's a way
to say, "I'm me, not just
a legacy." He wants to be
as dependable as the color
guard that marches before
the national anthem.

3.

"I had to hit the brakes
and he hit me from behind."
So much for the pole position.
He'll race, but regulations say

he'll start last in a car that
didn't run the time trials.
Not to worry, it's still plenty
fast. By mid-race, the crowd
rises to cheer as he takes
the lead, if only briefly.

4.

"This should be called
the Lotto 500," says the race
announcer, "It's so unpredictable."
So Jr. dodged and trained,
duct-taped and pit-stopped,
survives to darned near
the last lap, only to get bumped
into the wall — not even able
to finish — but given the odd
calculations of the sport, he's
listed 24th among 48 starters.
Yes, the crowd rose as one on
lap 3 to hold 3 fingers
up in honor of his dad, but
nothing is guaranteed. Jr.'s
already 36 and for now, he
has to wait 'til next year.

SHOOTOUT

Maybe they aren't guns,
but these cars are weapons —
hundreds of horsepower
burning through a gallon
in 2 minutes. Slap a wall —
you're lucky to shower
the track with sparks,
or spin and pray the cage
protects you. Straight
out, floored, pushing
cars nearly 200.

"Too dangerous," NASCAR
says and restricts the air flow.
"Just too fast." But fans
want a real race, flat out
toward the checkered flag.
All that skill, all that power —
no room for yellow here.
Only the flash of a green
flag, then hell-bent
toward victory, a show-
off lap, back slapping
and media hoopla.

In the summer of 2011, Danica Patrick committed to racing full time in NASCAR's Nationwide Series.

DANICA PATRICK

1. Political Correctness

Let's get the leering out of the way
right away, but it doesn't hurt that
she's really good looking. Still,
if a woman is going to race in what
is still a man's world, she'd better
be plenty tough about the comments.
We aren't that far from sexy pin-ups
on every mechanic's garage walls.

2. Ethnicity

In Serbian, it's DAN-ee-tsa.
Americans could probably learn
that, although she, herself, says,
"Dan-i-ka." Maybe because
in Serbia, they also still say,
"*Jena i jena*" — a woman is
a woman — as the caption for
a scantily-clad centerfold in
the daily news. That's a good
reason for a name to get
Americanized.

3. Winning Some Points at Least

Used to be green was an unlucky
color for a race car not to mention

the number 13. Used to be a woman
would never race. She entered 13
in 2010 and scheduled 12 for 2011.

Break a few rules, break a few
expectations. GoDaddy! Even her
sponsor is techy and new. Her first
year in NASCAR she racked up
enough points to beat 100 men.
Now she's signed on as a star.

TO BE COMPLETELY HONEST

"Don't bet on this sport," says Dale, Jr.,
who ought to know. "It's a lottery.
You just can't predict who'll win."
They've regulated so much about
the cars that they all look alike.
No wonder every bumper and grill
are a match — with templates enforced
to within 1/8th of an inch. The air
restrictor plates, carburetor settings,
the tires, suspension, not to mention
weight and fuel. All that's left
to chance is who's going to crash
out in the Big One. It's hard to hear
a driver say, for all his pluck, the sport
comes down to just dumb luck.
For all the talent and showy colors,
for all the pairing up for the dance,
you could be clever as a fox and
still lose. But hey, that's what we
love about America — just about
anyone has a chance.

THE POLITICS OF ETHANOL

(NASCAR's official fuel contains 15% ethanol.)

Let's burn food for fuel.
We have too many hungry
people. Some can starve —
economic survival of the fittest.

Turn corn into ethanol.
Push food prices up.
Pay no attention to that
man behind the screen
or all the studies that say
even large-scale production
isn't cost or energy efficient.

It isn't lack of oil forcing
us toward biofuel. It's
too much of it — too much
oil-industry power distracting
us from better batteries,
solar chargers, cheap,
powerful electric cars.

Don't get me started on
the lack of good mass transit
that would get people to work
without cars, so folks could make
a few dollars, feed their families
on cheaper food, the price
of which wouldn't be inflated
by making ethanol.

"AIN'T THAT WHAT IT'S ALL ABOUT?"

(For Waddell Wilson.)

"Speed never bothered me
none," says Waddell. "I
won me some pretty purses
before I figured engine
building was my niche."
109 wins later, 3 at
the 500, he's earned
his Legacy award. Over
200 mph? Sounds pretty
good to the old guys,
"Speed is what it's all
about." But NASCAR
wants it family-friendly.
It's tough to bring
the family to the track
to see a fellow hit the wall
and die. "I haven't built
a flathead in years. That's
what I used to race ... I won
a few but building them
is a lot safer than drivin' 'em."
Ah, but would he take the wheel
in one of those fancy cars?
"Guess I'm a bit past
doing it now," but still
strong-voiced and glad
for the Legacy honors.

SCORING

"So, if you win you get all the points?"
"No, you get extra points."
"And if you crash, you don't get any points?"
"No, you can get even more points than the guy who wins."
"But if you come in last, do you get any point?"
"A few."
"So, you get points if you crash or lose?"
"That's true."
"For pity's sake, tell me how they score."

"Any driver who leads a lap during a race receives
one bonus point. The driver who leads the most
laps receives an additional bonus point.
The race winner receives 3 bonus points."

"I guess I get it. If you run first for
lots of laps, then even if you crash
you can get a ton of points."

"Not quite. The winner gets 43 points
plus 3 bonus points, plus an extra point
for each lead lap, plus an extra point if
he leads for the most laps so he could
get a total of 48, or not …"

"Or not? But if there were a big crash
and the guy who was leading and a bunch
of others close behind couldn't finish …"

"Then, if the last-place guy somehow
got to win, he'd get 43 points plus

3 so he could get more than
the car that ran up-front for the race
and almost won."

"And this is the new scoring system
NASCAR says they've simplified?"

"True. Now, let me explain the other
rules about who gets guaranteed to start
or the way they pay out purses."

"Excuse me, but I'm going for nachos
and some aspirin."

Ray Fox (left) and Fireball Roberts are pictured on the cover of Ray's biography, written by Godwin Kelly, the Motorsports Editor for the *Daytona Beach News-Journal*.

RAY FOX

He doesn't think of himself as a pioneer,
though others say so. "We just had lots
of extra parts from Chevy so we built
3 cars" — in 1963 the first to race
3 at once at the 500. And as for inventing
drafting, "Jr. Johnson figured that out
when he raced for me." Ray Fox, at
95, is just a gentle giant, admitting
only that, "We sat on the pole and we
won a lot." An interviewer would like
him to reveal some secrets, remember
old grudges. "I only wish we had better
parts," says Ray, "If we turned over
8,000 rpms those valve springs would
break and that was it. We'd be
out of it." In those days, it was Ford
vs. Chevy. It must have been fierce —
somewhere between enemy camps
and corporate war. But Ray just says,
"We were competitive but we were
friends." His daughter remembers
some squabbles, but Ray is content,
"I don't want an old friend to hear
me going over that, and I don't want
any trouble with NASCAR."
It's men like Ray who built the sport,
and he's stayed with it to found
the Living Legends of Auto Racing
Museum. "He's always been a motorhead,"
his friend says. But nowadays, with
young drivers bragging and even
brawling, the way Ray sees it
sure sounds like wisdom.

AT THE LEGACY OF SPEED BANQUET

The collectors are out
with glossies, NASCAR
jackets, even model cars
to be signed. The old-timers
are glad to slap each
other's backs. Those
500s left you exhausted
and sore. Now it's a soft
seat and a slide show
you can pick your young
self out of, or shout,
"There's Billy! Gawd,
he was handsome!"

These are easy times,
showing up for kudos
and autographs. 3 drivers
from the '60s stand
close for a photo —
but this one is for themselves.
You can tell by their gentle
hands around the shoulders,
this one is sincere. Speed was
one thing. Now, they
take it all in stride, glad
they have survived.

AUTOGRAPHS

The principle is called "contagious magic."
Someone or something has special powers.
You touch and the powers transfer to you.
It's worked since you caught that homerun
ball at the big league game and touched it
before you batted on the little league team.
The rabbit's foot — another story. Not
so lucky for the rabbit but an ancient sign —
where there were rabbits, with luck you,
too, could find lots of food. So, you stand
in line to get the autograph. Others may
see it as a quick way to make a buck
selling on eBay, but you know better.
If you get a NASCAR champ to sign, it
has to bring you better luck. Your car
will always start. You'll get to work on time.
If you get a picture of you two shaking hands,
frame the photo for your desk. "Is that you
with Earnhardt?" You'll get promoted, a big
raise and finally you can buy those Daytona
500 Tower tickets that cost a fortune but
come with the chance to meet more
drivers, get more autographs, good luck,
and like magic, you are sure to win.

In a demolition derby, the last car still driving wins. The same rule often applies when cars the exit speedway parking lots.

DEMOLITION DERBY

Okay, admit it, you race nuts,
for all the speed, you love
the crashes. Not that anyone
wants a guy injured badly
but a broken bone is the price
athletes can pay, and when
6 or 10 cars begin to spin,
it's better than a pinball game
keeping those impacts going.

That's why the demolition derby
is my favorite event. No guilty
waiting for the crashes. Wham!
And wham again, and again,
toward the single objective —
to ruin your opponent's car.
Circle 'round to catch him broadside.
Cream him. Bash him. Mangulate
the sucker so you, steaming radiator,
stove-in doors, dragging that rear
bumper, are the last car still moving.

A SONNET FOR NASCAR

It's not a sport that smacks of intellect
but auto racing still deserves respect.
Let's face it, most of what an athlete does
is masochism or just dangerous.
The symbolism, racing 'round a track,
is that there is a chance we're coming back.
It may be that we lose and try again,
or maybe it's a record time and win.
Ecclesiastes speaks of vanity
but also hope. It tests our sanity
to sit for hours enduring noise and smoke
to see our favorite driver crash or choke.
Don't over-think the sport. Participate.
To be a NASCAR fan requires faith.

IT TAKES TWO

Training, pushing,
love bugging, drafting,
synchronized racing,
the old bump and push,
the new style, teaming,
partnering, the NASCAR tango.
"We don't know what
to call it yet," says
the sports announcer
when bumper to bumper
driving sweeps into the 500.
Faster, for the lack of drag;
faster, for 2 engines doubled up;
faster than NASCAR wants them
to go, and so — restrictor plates,
a smaller grill, a release valve
(a.k.a. trick radiator cap) that
blows if the engine gets too hot.
But hasn't anyone noticed
the driving style is what is dangerous?
Why not ban tandem racing —
no 2 cars can double up and push?
Get back to the real sport where
speed is what it's all about,
daring drivers in ever-faster cars
conquering endurance, speed
and curves to win the race.

Dale Earnhardt, Jr., driver of the #88 National Guard/AMP Energy Chevrolet, is pushed by Kasey Kahne, driver of the #4 Red Bull Toyota, and Clint Bowyer, driver of the #33 Cheerios Chevrolet, is pushed by Jeff Burton, driver of the #31 Caterpillar Chevrolet, during the NASCAR Sprint Cup Series 2011 Daytona 500.

BUMPER TO BUMPER

They haven't quite named it
yet but they're doing it —
closer than lovers or at least
faster, pressing so close it's
dangerous. Waltrip, Logano,
Busch and Biffle — in one race
10 in all — going over 200 mph,
pulses racing toward record speeds.
Once, air resistance called for stream-
lining and spoilers that conquered
unwanted lift. Train-drafting
cut more off the time. No more
high-seated, goggled, grinning
show offs racing out ahead
of the pack. Now, drivers
couple up and tunnel through
straightaways and curves.
But this new pavement,
asphalt that grips back
at tires like a lover licking
skin — the closer you can follow,
bumper to bumper, the more
speed, and the more likely
you will win.

The pit crews, arguably, work harder than the drivers. This photo was taken at the NASCAR Labor Day race weekend at the Auto Club Speedway, Fontana, CA.

IN THE GARAGES

1. The Talent and the Crew

He arrives in his gray sweats, a Coke
in hand, his logo-hat tilted sideways —
the talent — as if showing up were work.
8 crew members have sweated all day,
pushing the car from inspection
to inspection. He's here to say hello,
sign a few autographs, take photos
with fans and friends. Tomorrow,
he'll drive for glory, but right now
he has to rush off for an interview.
The crew, dressed as a team,
go back to work as usual.

2. Exhaust

It's all you can do to hold
your breath but why would
you want to? A wave of hot
exhaust catches you and you
breathe deeply. They say
the monoxide that can
kill you has no odor.
Ethylenes cause cancer.
But for real race nuts,
that smell is perfume.

3. Recycling

A member of the pit crew leaves
the garage, walking all but on
tiptoes, balancing 2 quarts
of spent oil in a deep pan.
Notice, there's not a spot
on the garage floor, nothing
vaguely greasy under the hood,
as a white-shirted official inspects
the car. The oil is bound for
the recycle station. If a drop
hits the ground, the EPA will
declare a state of emergency.

4. Tire Man

You only get 6 for the whole race —
that's for practice, blowouts, the whole
week. They regulate them so carefully
you don't get much choice:

	Left Front	Right	Left Rear	Right
Rollout	87.9 in.	88.5 in.	87.9 in.	88.5 in.
Weight	24.3 lbs.	24.4 lbs.	24.3 lbs.	24.4 lbs.
Width	10.6 in.	10.8 in.	10.6 in.	10.8 in.
Life	250 mi.	125 mi.	250 mi.	125 mi.

Not cheap. About $400 for each tire.
So, he's measuring each with a yellow
chalked string to get the exact diameter
on center. These are his babies, filled
with pure nitrogen to a pressure only he

knows so they'll grip great and wear long.
A blowout is usually a crash out. Sometimes,
he wishes the tanks held nitrous oxide.

5. Fueling for a Test Run

He wraps his arms around the gas can
like he's lifting something precious.
It's just half full, 6 gallons, but it weighs
over 50 pounds. He's quick to find the mouth,
delivering the bluish fuel as fast as gravity
lets it flow. After, he wipes the mouth with
a soft rag. He'd burp the baby but
it weighs 3,400 pounds.

Greg Biffle's car gets inspected before qualifying for the Sylvania 300 at the New Hampshire Motor Speedway.

BODY MAN

I'm working this rubber hammer,
thumping like a bass drum in a marching
band. It was that brush against the wall
a race ago. Now everything is out of kilter.
I could have changed the bumper, but
I thought I had it right in the shop.
So they let us out of the inspection line
to whack at it. First, there was the template
over the roof. We passed that fine.
There are 20 officials measuring me
down to 1/8th of an inch. They got us
on a quarter panel but I'm the guy
they call the interrogator because I
turn the thumbscrews and torture
a car back into shape. Then, they
get us on the front bumper. Man,
it just won't line up for the template.
Funny thing is, later, we'll be squirting
WD-40 on it so we can slide right up
and push. At 190 mph you sure don't
want any friction so, just as well
we fix it here and now.

WHAT'S ON THE HOOD

1.

Landon Cassill says, "Thank a teacher."
His apple-red car could be the gift
that raises him a grade.

2.

Who can argue with Danica?
"GoDaddy!"

3.

Tony Stewart's racing for Burger King.
His crewman wears the emblem on a big
pot belly. Too many Whoppers?

4.

Missing, a mother and daughter,
Diane and Tammy, just 16.
Gone since 1979.

Call if you have any information.

Kevin Conway put it on his car
because the family never got
an answer about what happened.
"They went out the door
and we never seen them again."

IT AIN'T JUST "OLD BOYS"

Sure, you can shout about the stereotypes,
pickup trucks and gun racks, folks who
won't stop fighting the Civil War, but
sports broke more color barriers than
people know and NASCAR isn't only
lily white. Elias Bowie went first,
granted, in 1955; then Charlie Scott,
finishing a respectable Grand National
in Daytona. Wendell Scott (same last
name but no relation) ran 495 Cup races
over 13 years. So don't tell me it can't
be done. More recently, Tibbs and Lester.
It's the 21st Century, folks, just waiting
for initiative — and a big-money sponsor
because let's face it, racing isn't cheap.
Then, there are Hispanics — nearly 1 in 10
of NASCAR's fans, not to mention
a Spanish-language website. Grow up
sports fans — it's America, land of the free —
where race relations only have to do
with your not pushing your fellow driver
into a spin on any given curve.

SPEEDWAY HAIKUS

*(A haiku is a 3-line picture-poem arranged
as 5, 7 and 5 syllables.)*

PIT CREW

taco in toolbox
waiting with one large bite mark
carburetor failed

IN THE OLD DAYS

we ran till we were
out of money, out of gas
and our tires went flat

LOVE BUGS

vegetable oil
on our front and back bumpers
next KY jelly

FAN GRAFFITI

Dale Earnhardt, Jr.
you can call my wife Sue Ann
she's got permission

MANQUE

pictures of headlights
paint-on grills replace real parts
cars left blind and mute

NASCAR CAMP GROUNDS

plastic wading pools
phone ringtones playing Dixie
barbecue and beer

NEW BALD TIRES

racing tires are bald
as a baby's ass except
for those rubber hairs

EARS

old mechanics go
without large orange ear plugs
they're already deaf

SCANNERS

like an old party line
you listen in on 10 guys
bragging who they'll date

RICHARD PETTY'S PROMISE

he promised his ma
he wouldn't endorse liquor
so no Busch Series

PICNIC BY THE RIG

20 pounds of ice
a case of beer but don't cook
too near the race fuel

TANDEM RACING

they head in the pits
together like women go
to the powder room

STILL OF USE

serious damage
put him 4 laps behind but
he's pushing someone

IN THE FAST LANE

laps like clock hands turn
50 seconds per minute
drivers live fast lives.

WORKING AT THE SPEEDWAY

1.

It's been nearly 2 years since the shop
closed. I haven't had regular work since
but they hired near 500 of us and trained
us locals for race week. If I stand, my
back hurts but if I sit, my circulation's
so poor my legs go to sleep. I ought to
lose some of this weight. But I can
do this — checking tickets for the tram.
Maybe I can come current on my rent.

2.

I played golf with some raceway fellows
and they said, "Hey, you're a photographer.
We can use you." Now, it's been 6 years
and I've got this great gig. Look at me,
walking around with a hot pass, big lens,
and I get all these great pictures of cars,
drivers — all the race action. Who would
have thought golf could do that? But hey,
it's a game presidents play.

3.

I'm here as a volunteer. We are a fast-
pitch softball travel team and every cent
we take in goes to the team. They gave us
this vendor cart. I know $4 is a lot for just
a Coke, but it's for charity. Sunscreen, sun-
screen, sunscreen and at least I get all I
want to drink for free. It's really fun for me.
Oh, I'm not a pitcher. I play right field.

According to *The Boston Phoenix*, the Collings Foundation holds an annual "Race of the Century." Here, a 1904 Franklin Type A Roadster races a horse and buggy. The Roadster, with a top speed of 12 mph, lost.

THE HORSE vs. THE RACE CAR

There are still men who wear
livery, walking their snorting
steeds slowly from the paddock,
tugging firmly on the bridle.
Jockeys mount confidently
for an exercise run.

There are stable hands
for mucking or just
walking behind the horse.

Here it's 6 guys in uniforms
silently rolling a car toward
the long wait for time trials.
Later, their driver slips through
a window, revs it up, screeching
for a pole position.

Then, there are the men
who run out to clear
the debris and clean
the mess that cars make.

SOUVENIRS

1.

After hours in the steaming
heat, the store air conditioning
tempts even the brokest fan.
Just walk in, cool down,
take a stroll around. Then,
bam, it's, "I've got to
have it," and you're all
grown up, so you don't even
have to beg your parents.
Just step out a moment
to check the ATM, wipe
the condensation off your
sunglasses, punch in your
PIN. The credit card is
already maxed but, "Yup,
I've got some bucks in
checking," so ka-ching —
cash money to go back
in and buy that NASCAR
cup and T-shirt.

2.

There's something about the
square Miller Lite hat that sells.
It looks like a 6-pack on your head.
Or the pink, collared Speedway
shirt that mom could wear. Hot
as it is, the authentic driver's jacket
would look so good when you
wear it in the fall. Or, how about
at least a beer mug and RACE CAR
PARKING ONLY sign? Sure,
you've got to carry them around
for the whole race. But heck, you
paid a fortune to get here.
Bring something back to
show your friends.

Fans cheer Dale, Jr. as he is introduced at the Coke Zero 400 at the Daytona Speedway.

A DOZEN FAN POEMS

1. Fan Participation

"Southern Pride," tattooed
atop his shoulders under
his muscle shirt. A square
Miller Lite hat gives him
a 6-pack head. He's up
on stage to play for prizes.
"You know what to do?"
asks the emcee. "Haven't
got a clue," he drawls
straight from the hills
of northern Georgia.
But he's got a knack —
balancing 6 chocolate
cupcakes on his forehead
so he can spin a wheel
of fortune and win
a Diecast metal race car.

2. Ronny and Jan

They were married on
the start-finish line
right after the Daytona 400.
Took their vows, crossed
over to start their later
lives as surely as Coke
Zero replaced Pepsi. Both
had been around before
but this one would be
the charm. After the ceremony
all the Earnhardts greeted them,

"Treated us like family."
They come back every July
to celebrate. "This way we
can't forget our anniversary."

3. I'm so Happy

There he is coming out
of the men's room. I make
a beeline right up to him
and pull off my hat. He
doesn't stop but takes it
right out of my hands
and signs it. Dale, Jr.
signed my hat. Oh,
my God, I'm so happy.
Look at me. I'm shaking.
Let me dial, "Mom?
No, I'm okay. Dale,
Jr. signed my hat.
I'm so happy. Look
at me, I'm shaking."

4. He Says It's for His Son

"I get to take trips with him.
We're collecting racetracks.
Been doing it since he turned
8 and now he's 16. A trip
a year is all we can afford."
They've worked their way
across the states nearer to
Colorado. Now, it's the East,
starting with Daytona.
"I think this is our favorite,"
he says, forgetting to ask his son.

5. Young Dad

He's pushing one son in
a stroller, another is tugging
at his hand. The 7-year-
old needs keeping an eye on.
But dad is sliding through
cell phone photos as he walks.
"Look at this one of pit row.
Isn't it cool?" His 3-year-old
isn't interested and the bigger
boy is way too far ahead.

6. Elegant

She looks well into her 70s,
well-styled, short white hair,
matching pink pedal pushers
and blouse with NASCAR
emblems. White NASCAR
tote bag over her shoulder.
A driver's mother? An official's
wife? Her credentials say, "HOT."

7. The Go-Kart Kid

So this little kid — maybe he's 8
and weighs 50 pounds — comes into
the 7-Eleven all done up in his driver's
suit and carrying a 10-pound helmet.
He's there for his Powerade and
some beef jerky for energy while
he waits for his heat. I ask him,
"Who's your favorite driver?"
The kid's no fool. "Me," he
says, "and I'm going to win."

8. Enthusiasm vs. Gravity

The lady in the powder-blue
tank top keeps standing to cheer
her driver every lap. For all
the rolls of dappled flesh
pushing from under her shirt,
she sure could use the exercise.
Between cheers she swigs her
beers, leaving fans to wonder
which will win out, enthusiasm
or the drink. By lap 20, she's
slower to stand. At 30, she
hollers maybe every other
lap. By 50 it's clear she's done,
rising only to make a pit stop.
It's probably the beer, or
maybe that her favorite
car is running 41st.

9. Two Brothers

2 young brothers, built
like tanks, in matching
Truck Series shirts, hold
big bags bulging with souvenirs.
The older bumps his brother
out of the way. 10 and he's
already learned how to race.

10. A Lull in the Action

Halfway through the race
the crowd grows quiet, glad

for full speed, no long cautions.
400, 500, 600 miles takes so long
to run. This way the race may
end sooner. All the drivers say
it really comes down to the last
laps, except, a big crash would
sure wake things up again.

11. Sheer Joy

"This is it," the M&M fan declares,
standing, turning to face the gathering
fans. "This is wonderful," he shouts.
The weather is gorgeous. The stands
are quickly filling. He's bought
himself a fancy seat, 10 rows up
near the start-finish line. Of course,
he's in full regalia, looking like
at least a member of the Busch
team, if not Kyle. "Don't you
just love this?" he shouts, tossing
his arms up. Folks catch his joy,
answering, "Hey M&M, you rock."
He rises again, to take a bow.
Later, who knows who planned it,
a half dozen small bags of M&Ms
rain down on him. And what does
he do? What else? He shares them.

12. The Magic Number

171,000 in attendance
for the Daytona 500.
Need we say more?

THE SUITS

Young marketing execs
in suits stepped in but
they forgot their roots,
big on building new
markets. See them
sending their limo drivers
to park in the executive
lot while they dine on
caviar and steak, looking
for the next big marketing
break. Maybe negotiations
for what — an opera presentation?

The fans drive their RVs
from the Carolinas, stopping
to eat at truck stops and diners.
They're what NASCAR is all
about, giving their favorite driver
a rebel shout, loyal to the core.
Hey, marketing boys, better go
back to the Grand Ole Opry.

MILKSHAKES

(In memory of Dan Wheldon.)

When I was a kid, they told us
drink a quart of milk a day
and you'll grow up big and strong.
Rich men drank scotch and most
guys drank beer, but for a race
win you celebrated with a bottle
of champagne popped open
at the finish and shaken to spray
the head, face and everyone.
Now, there's Dan Wheldon
dumping milk on himself,
jumping up and down as if
he were some kind of milkshake.
Yes, there's the kid who won
the 500. He just turned 20,
so he had no choice. Hershey
may put his picture on their
chocolate milk. But victory
lane without champagne?
Whatever they do at the Indy,
at NASCAR it's not the same.
If you drink all that milk as a kid,
you should have something with
a kick to celebrate your new fame.

DISAPPOINTMENT

It's a sport for real men, brave
men. Don't lose your cool. Don't
let it show. But all that work.
For what? Stress in the garage —
just a fire under your skin.
Anger when it isn't ready yet —
awake at 2 a.m. waiting for daylight.
Nerves before the race —
adrenalin, that makes you ready
for the fight. The green flag,
then, not half way through
the race, some fool ahead of you
hits his brakes and you bump him,
crash out. You'll ache tomorrow,
a belt bruise across your
shoulder like a tattoo.
Only now, that tightness
in your chest, just where you
swallow, and you know what
it is — disappointment. Okay,
anxiety. It only hits you when
there's absolutely nothing
you can do. Helpless as
a novice. All that time,
effort, money; all those
hopes. It's like picturing
the perfect finish and then,
instead, getting to see
what your end will be.

THANKS TO DOPPLER

Nothing passed ancient observers
rapidly enough for them to notice
a change in pitch. Sounds came
at them as if the air were angry,
signaling something likely
dangerous, and once past,
one could heave a sigh of relief.

We had to wait for fast conveyances,
sirens blaring, or trains with obligatory
whistles sounding, before Doppler
noticed: first, a rising pitch; then
as quickly, a falling off.

He calculated the compression
of waves, the consequent higher
frequency, the corollary stretching
out and lowering pitch of objects
moving away. He even applied
this to the movement of the stars.

Thus, reassured, when blaring
somewhere raises our attention,
forcing us to calculate whether
it is coming or going, or when
a race car roars by us, its fierce
shriek subsiding, we can thank
Doppler, not to mention that
the monster did not eat us.

Colin Braun, Steve Wallace and Brian Scott, tangle up in turn 2 during the Scotts Turf Builder 300 race at the Bristol Motor Speedway.

THE BALLAD OF THE STOCK CAR RACES

Some say it takes real skill to win.
Some say it ain't worth trying.
I say a bit of each is true
plus there's a chance of dying.

The sport is more a rich man's game.
The cost is stupefying.
If you want to form a race car team,
the poor are not applying.

There's licensing and packaging
and who will be your sponsor.
I'll spare you all the business stuff.
Let legal give that advice, sir.

Some say it takes real skill to win.
Some say it ain't worth trying.
I say a bit of each is true
plus there's a chance of dying.

Think who will build and race the car,
the driver and pit crew.
Think long and hard about how far
your choice is going to get you.

You could go with some old codger who
built good straight-8 engines
or buy a fancy engineer
who'll come up with new inventions.

Some say it takes real skill to win.
Some say it ain't worth trying.
I say a bit of each is true
plus there's a chance of dying.

I'd look for that combination, rare
but clearly something doable—
a natural born mechanic who
makes every bolt unscrewable.

He's got to know an engine well
and also be tech savvy.
The days of monkey grease are gone.
It's gotten pretty fancy.

Some say it takes real skill to win.
Some say it ain't worth trying.
I say a bit of each is true
plus there's a chance of dying.

I have a feeling folks will laugh
but let some color splatter.
Publicize a cause or 2.
What's on your hood can matter.

Sure, the sponsors cover the cars.
Sure, there are lucky numbers,
but if you're racing for your dad
there's more between the bumpers.

Some say it takes real skill to win.
Some say it ain't worth trying.
I say a bit of each is true
plus there's a chance of dying.

Once your mission has been set
and once you bring the crew on,
once you reinforce the car
and drop in that big engine,

there's still the driver you will field.
What's in his heart does matter.
A bragging brat may also win,
but there's more to a race than chatter.

> *Some say it takes real skill to win.*
> *Some say it ain't worth trying.*
> *I say a bit of each is true*
> *plus there's a chance of dying.*

I'd pick a driver from mid-range
who's wracked up points to prove things —
5 or 8 years of driving hard
but never quite the top wins.

That makes him hard and hungry so
he'll drive like hell but listen.
Give him a car and spotter team.
He'll find the groove and glisten.

> *Some say it takes real skill to win.*
> *Some say it ain't worth trying.*
> *I say a bit of each is true*
> *plus there's a chance of dying.*

Top speed's a matter of building right.
Your shape is predetermined.
Pit crews can practice until they break.
Your driver should be unswerving.

If he waits a second in a curve,
or goes high instead of dropping,
it's a game of chicken on the track
and fenders could be popping.

> *Some say it takes real skill to win.*
> *Some say it ain't worth trying.*
> *I say a bit of each is true*
> *plus there's a chance of dying.*

"Go high, go low, there's a spin, go slow.
You're talking in his helmet.
There's a calculator in his brain
and that's what's got to help him.

You don't get that from school or talk.
It isn't from a textbook.
That's where his guts and instinct rule
and winning is just hell bent.

> *Some say it takes real skill to win.*
> *Some say it ain't worth trying.*
> *I say a bit of each is true*
> *plus there's a chance of dying.*

Open throttle, heart and mind —
it may sound sentimental.
For all the metal and the cash,
winning is something mental.

You've got your sponsors, marketers,
mechanics and the pit crew,
the fuel, the tires, the special struts,
and who will drive for you.

Then there's dumb luck. To win a race
it's equal skill and fate.
A favorite spins and hits the wall.
Fast cars can't keep the pace,

or time it wrong, run out of gas.
Pole cars can finish last.
For all the planning and the tasks,
history is just the past.

The driver has to be first class
to win in it all in NASCAR.

Some say it takes real skill to win.
There is a chance of dying.
I say a bit of each is true
but winning is worth trying.

TO DIE FOR

*(The Richard Petty Driving Experience lets regular folks drive
a NASCAR race car.)*

Just the sound of it — that roar
that could kill your hearing
when you open it up on
the track; even taking a minute
and a half for each lap makes
your head spin and heart
jump. This is not for chickens,
curves happening faster than
any normal driver can react
and you with your hand on
the shift, a foot poised over
the clutch but barely time
to downshift. Imagine 200
laps of this with 30 or 40 other
cars close enough to touch
but touching could be fatal.
You heard your driving coach:
"Don't screw around out there."
But just once you want to
drop down like a pro on
that inside turn, head into
the straightaway floored.
They've put a governor on it
so you can't do something
stupid, but for what you paid,
what the hell. When will
you ever do this again? It's
something a fan could die for.

SNEAKING

(For Bruce Moran, who watched them build the Speedway.)

Before the track got built
my dad was on to Bill France's
tricks. Sure it scared me when
he brought me to those thick
saw palmettos along the beach.
There was that sign, clear
as day, saying "Danger!
Rattle Snakes." "No such thing,"
dad said, "It's to keep the dumb
ones out." So we pushed through
to a great spot to sneak to
watch the races.

When they opened the Speedway
in 1959, my buddies and I were
ready. We drove an old Ford
pickup, with a wheelbase wide
and high enough to get through
swampy spots and make our own
little road to the pine trees outside
the southwest curve. For days
we climbed the trees and built
a platform where we could see
out across the back straightaway.
France and his friends were
doing big business by then.
But not everyone had $20 for
a fancy ticket and we watched that
first 500 from start to finish, free.

HOW GRANNY LEARNED TO LOVE NASCAR

Granny — we call her Grams —
never was a fan of racing
but she was curious why
we all got so darned excited so
when the track offered a free
go-see before the big race, she
up and said, "Bring me."
We gave her a boost into
the pickup and drove her
there on a day so sunny
it'd make a mole smile.

Grams walked real slow.
She never was one to want
a wheel chair — said it would
be like a mule in mud which
wouldn't be so bad for most
mules, but she had this mule,
Agnes she called her, after
her mother-in-law, Agnes,
who died cause she was
so stubborn she wouldn't
wear shoes in any weather
so when a cotton-mouthed
water moccasins bit her big
toe she never even told no one
so she just lay there and died.

Anyway, Gram's mule, Agnes,
she was a mule wouldn't
get her hooves muddy

no matter what, so Grams
wasn't going to use no
wheelchair. She just made
her own way slow to the stands
with her hickory cane knocking.
Grams has trouble hearing.
It's somewhere between asking,
"Huh what?" till we're crazy
or her not giving a darn what
we say — but there was such
a heck of a roar from the track
it did make her walk a little faster.
When she got up that ramp
to the edge of the 4th turn,
she fixed her face to the fence
to watch and even the fellow
whose job it was to make folks
"Stand back," didn't have
the heart to chase her.

Then, from way back around
the curve comes this red Monte
Carlo screaming like a charging
pig — wildest thing — probably
near 200 mph. Gram stood right
up there, eyes fixed straight on
it coming right at her. She never
nearly even ducked. Then, she
turns to us with a giddy grin,
and says, "Get me a ticket
to them races."

CARS, MOTORCYCLES AND MAN CAVES

Say what you want about equality of the sexes,
you don't have to be Sigmund Freud to know
there's something going on with men and cars.
They aren't "hidden persuaders" — big engines
roaring down straightaways, drivers entering
an apex — that's just a turn-on. Then, there's
the sheer abandon — beyond an actor's
butterflies or some bungee-jumper's nerve.
Even on a 31° embankment, at close to
180, if you go wide, it still feels like
you'll fly off the curve. Take away
all the protection — straddling a 1000cc
bike, knee puck extended to graze
the ground — that's a bigger high than Everest.
Then, there are those days just working in
the garage, the ultimate man cave, bedecked
with posters of hero drivers, legendary cars,
and yes, those pictures of scantily clad girls.

IN PERSPECTIVE

The Goodyear blimp
circles the Speedway
while fans hurry to
the track and stands.

In empty lots for
miles, campers cue up
for spaces. Even trans-
port trucks, unloaded,
convert to homes
for crews and fans.

A crowd for time
trials pins them-
selves to trackside fences
despite "No Stopping
Along the Fence" signs
warning of ever-
present danger.

500 feet above,
in a gondola slipping
smoothly through
a bright blue sky, folks
could wonder, "What's
the big hurry?"

THERE'S ALWAYS A PIGEON

This one is undistinguishable
from a million others except
it's perched on a pole by
the flag tower overhanging
the track and, as cars roar
by below, it barely ruffles
a feather, accustomed
to these objects flying by.
Only a spill of Nachos
sets it in flight as a fan
loses $8 worth of goodies
and a 4th-place car
makes an inside move
into third on a curve.

OUT OF GAS

1. Dale Earnhardt, Jr. at the Coke 600

It's longest race that NASCAR runs.
You've been driving nearly 5 hours
and it comes to this. You've chased
down 2 leaders in the final 20 laps
to take the lead. You've argued
with your crew chief over whether
to pit for fuel. You got a great jump
off a late-lap pile-up that put you
into first. 150 gallons of 98-octane
gas, guzzled in a grind that tested
strategy as much as nerve, letting
others burn their maximum as you
laid back, coasted, waited for them
to pit — even for a few seconds so
you could win this. It seemed like
a good gamble. "I just did what my
dang chief said," you tell us later.
But a half lap from the finish —
as your fans are jumping up
and down that you will win — you
run out of gas, letting 6 cars race
by as you coast in for 7th, which is,
you say, "better than crashing out."

2. When I was a Teen

First you picked her up at her house
and heard her father's rules:
"You kids be good. None of that
nonsense. Just see your movie and
get her back on time. 11 p.m., that's
it." Then it was McDonalds, a zombie
movie and just enough little kisses
and tickles that you were both
turned on. Sure, it was an old trick,
but driving home the long way,
you'd sneak a hand to the key
and turn the engine off, declaring,
"Oh darn, I think we're out of gas."
And if she believed it, you could
just sit there in the dark, sigh
loudly and see what happened.
Or at least that was how it used to
work. Now, before you could even
move closer to her on the seat,
she'd be texting her girlfriends,
"OMG he says we're out of gas.
Does he think I'm dumb." Then
its all over Twitter. She's posting
you looking stupid on Facebook.
She reaches for the key, starts
the engine. You drive home wishing
for the good old days when girls
were innocent or pretended that
they were fooled.

3. Anywhere U.S.A.

Nothing sadder than a man
on the roadside, gas cap open,
staring uselessly into that black
fill hole. No great quest to strike
oil, drill rig churning while
a crew and investors await
the gush, as in some old film.
Just a gray-faced man, annoyed
he's let his AAA lapse. His buddy
says he'll be there with a can
of gas, but when? He scowls
at his cotton jacket — too light
for a chilly autumn night.
Nothing to do but wait. A car
is nothing to hate, though
it does feel good to kick it.

OLD DRIVERS NEVER DIE

They just need more pit stops.
They just slip their clutches.
They just join the pit crew.
They just lose their sponsors.
They just run down to flat.
They just sit and idle.
They just run out of gas.

Gas cans and tires

GROWING UP
WITH CARS AND RACING

Sam Axelrod made himself a souped up golf cart to drive the
Cape Ann golf course in Essex, MA.

A HISTORY OF SPEED

When I was little, I wondered why
my father didn't speed. We'd go
on errands and he'd let so many
cars go past him. Weren't we
supposed to win the race?

Then, there was that silver
door handle and something
told me to pull on it. When
the rear car door swung open,
it took half a block for my
dad to stop after I fell out.

Ever since I can remember I
wanted to drive. I'd sit on
dad's lap and steer while he
worked the pedals. I knew
you didn't have to pull on
the wheel — just hold it
steady — but I sure liked
those loops we made
in the parking lot.

When we visited the farm,
at least I got to start
the tractor — even roll
into the field. But what
good is a big engine if
you don't get up speed?

Going to driving school

was required to get a license.
I guess hearing all those
safety things was okay,
but all I wanted was to get
behind the wheel — not
talk about it.

14. Florida still gave a kid
a license at 14. How cool
was that? But mostly I still
drove with a parent in the car
so no chance to wind out
or see what the numbers at
the top of the dial felt like.

16 and I got the keys to solo.
Even took it on the highway
but I was more scared of tickets
than crashing. My father
would have killed me for
speeding. So, just 55.

18 and the new interstate let
us go 65. That meant 70 or
even 75 except that new radar
detector thing made it easier
for troopers so my first long
trip was pretty tame. Besides,
the Studebaker Lark showed
120 for a top speed but it
felt like it would come apart
if I tried to hit 90.

Oh, but my new Cutlass could
really fly, and there I was
alone, out in the passing lane
in Georgia, when a local cop
got me: "Doing 92, son.
You're under arrest so
just follow me up the road
to the court house." It didn't
matter to me that his brother
was the judge. He had me
dead to rights so I didn't argue.
I just paid the fine and limped
off in my yellow, targa-top
Olds with the New York plate.
And I wonder why he
picked me to ticket?

After I solved some wiring
problems, reworked and tuned
the engine, I took my 442 out
for a test drive. Finally! Triple
digits. I'm going to guess 135,
though its speedometer
topped off at 120. You figure —
a 451 engine in a light-weight
car. I guess I got the jones for
speed then — or maybe it was
just sitting in the back seat
while my daddy drove and I
thought every time we went
somewhere it was a race
not just driving to get there.

ON MY OWN

I tag after my dad, hoping
not to get lost among
the throng of strangers
at West Peabody Speedway
where he greets friends
and admires modified stock
cars. He's ready to grab
a wrench, ready to crew.
I'm sure I'd like to be like him —
able to fix engines and everything,
Only, he says tonight is too
hot for a 5-year-old to hold
his dad's hand. I'm standing
on my own amid revving engines,
short bursts of spinning wheels,
men swearing and hollering.
It's that same night a car
throws a wheel into the crowd
and I see a spectator get killed.
My dad hurries me home
after that, holding my hand
all the way to his truck
in the parking lot.

ROCKY

It was my older brother's Soap Box
Derby racer, but I went along to
watch him compete. He'd smoothed
his wooden hood, painted 4 coats
of shiny red lacquer and planned
where to put his trophy.

The official starter was Rocky
Marciano, the "Brockton Bomber,"
and a model for any poor kid who
wanted to fight his way to the top.
Rocky had won 43 in a row,
undefeated and new world champ.

I was maybe 8 or 9, a little kid
with not much muscle, so when
he stopped to shake my hand
as I shoved it toward him walking
toward the starting line, he
scared me when he reached to grab it.

His hand was the largest I had
ever seen — disappearing mine in
a massive squeeze of knuckles.
He smiled and walked along. I
looked at what was left — my
wrung-out, small white paw —
and promised I would never
wash that hand.

MA'S MYSTERY NOISE

Mechanics joke about noises
customers make to say why
they brought their car in.
My mother made her noise when
my dad came home from his
garage. He'd have laughed at
her but there was that day
the steering wheel came off
in her hands as she pulled out
in traffic, so he figured this time
he'd better listen. He was the one
who had worked on the steering
column and then sent her off
on errands. "So what does
it sound like?" he encouraged.
"It's a rapid tapping, tapping,
tapping," ma said, clicking her
nails on the kitchen table.
"Probably the tappets," dad
said, and my mother got angry.

He disappeared downstairs to
test drive; came back an hour
later and declared. "Fixed."
Next day, when he came home
from work she gave it to him
good. "Not fixed," she said,
and you spend hours doing
jobs so everyone else's car
is perfect. What about
mine?" Another hour before
he could sit for supper — dutifully
out in the yard, leaning over

a fender on an old army blanket
so he wouldn't get grease on ma's
white convertible. "Fixed," he sighed
when he came back in. But,
do I have to tell you this went
on for 2 more days? Until,
ma declared him either deaf
or dumb because he said he
couldn't hear any noise and
she said he hadn't fixed it.

"Everyone up," my dad
hollered. "Everyone into
the car." Which was just my
brother, my ma and me,
but we 3 marched with him
to the car and climbed in. He
started the engine, pulled out
quickly from the driveway and
took us to a smooth road nearby.
"Hear that? Hear that tapping?"
my mother insisted. None of us
did. Then, as my mother turned
to enlist us in the back seat, I
saw my dad put it in neutral
and turn off the engine. "I think
I hear the engine tapping now,"
he said. "Yes, yes. That's it,"
my ma said, "Now fix it." What
my dad did under the hood
when we got home, I'll never
know, but my mother was so
pleased he finally fixed it, she
baked him an apple pie.

THE EXTINCTION OF THE GREASE MONKEY

Dad used to dump his old oil down
the big slate sink in the garage.
At the junkyard, he'd cut up cars
on dirt so packed with grease it
was like blacktop. Sure, we loved
the earth and sea. They were big,
welcoming, and endlessly forgiving.
Except for that canal by the leather
factory that stank of sulfur and death,
but a pan of old black oil? That came
from caring for your car, giving it
its new life-blood. If dad gave me
the job, I'd even dip a finger in
to smear a black spot on each cheek
like war paint. Then, I'd pour it
down the drain, returning it to nature.

SANDSOAP

That grime gets in your skin,
not to mention into the cuts
on your knuckles skinned pulling
on a Snap-on wrench that popped.
A palm reader could predict
a gusher with all the oil soaking
your lifelines. Get out the GoJo
with its fine pumice and degreaser
and, okay, a little lanolin to smooth
away a day spent fiddling with
the carburetor, fighting with hoses,
tweaking the suspension. But
nothing can get the grease out
from under those fingernails.

Buggy racing, shown artfully in this fantasy photo, was my sport of choice when I was a kid. NASCAR has made the All-American Soap Box Derby part of its Youth Initiative.

BUGGY RACING

Memorial Day, my friends, Al, Bion
and I sat on the stone wall in front
of my house on Cabot Street to watch
the big parade that started just
blocks from us at Balch Playground.
It was a brilliant, sunny day,
reminding us of school's end
less than a month away.
The holiday was not to remember
soldiers who had died. In 1953,
we thought of all the heroes we knew,
who'd fought in WWII in the Pacific,
like Buzzy Branch's father, who kept
a bottle on the mantel with 2
enemy ears afloat in formaldehyde.

The Beverly High School Band led off,
followed by the National Guard
with polished shoes and hup 2-3s,
artillery and jeeps. Then, St. Mary's
Crusaders Marching Band, prized
throughout the State, with premier
twirler, Linda Towers, at the front
tossing her baton 20 feet
into the air just when she saw us.
Her brother, Bobby, told me she
practiced 6 hours every day
to learn it — a double spin-around
and blind catch behind her back.
Her hair in blond banana curls,
her pink underpants showing

as she spun, her fur-tufted boots.
After the parade, we ran to our
backyards to build new buggies —
our versions of Soap Box Derby racers,
only we used orange crates for hoods,
each pine board and blue-steel
flathead nail carefully removed,
saved for reuse. The labels,
with their bright designs — too-orange
oranges beneath a California sun —
we peeled away to shape the end boards
into rounded hoods; a winged Mercury,
stolen from the local junkyard,
ornamenting our accomplishments.
Up the Welden's long tar drive
we pulled them to test their rubber
baby-carriage wheels, bearings
packed lovingly with thick, black
grease. To steer, we tied a clothes-
line to a 2x4 bolted to the front,
the axle held on by big, bent-over
spikes. For brakes, a stick
to drag a tire or the ground.

Just then, we heard the sirens
rushing to somewhere near our street.
We might have run to see what,
but it was dusk, a school night
and we had to go in. Next morning,
the *Beverly Times* headlined,
TOWERS GIRL KILLED INSTANTLY
when a car struck her bicycle
on Cabot Street. The driver
said he couldn't see her, lost
in the glare of a large, red

setting sun. In school, they
asked us to say a special prayer.
Friday that week, the paper
said her funeral had 100
cars but my friends and I
couldn't attend. We had to
stay in school.

By the weekend, it was off to race
our buggies on the perfect hill.
Not Swan Street on the corner
where I lived — a contradiction
of its name, unsleek, unsmooth —
or other streets near ours,
their tar-and-bluestone surfaces
retarding speed. Not Welden's
or any of the driveways of my friends,
which, if smooth, were only modest
slopes that let us listen for any
grinding in the wheels. We sought
the longest, steepest, smoothest,
newly black-topped hill and found it,
2 miles away — the private road
right through the Catholic cemetery,
tucked safely away from traffic,
well worth a long, hot walk
with car in tow.

It was hot that Saturday —
just one week past Memorial Day
and already 80. We took the shortcut,
a back road over Reservoir Hill,
past the dirt embankments
and artificial pond where we caught
golden carp or perch on wooden poles

with rusting hooks — a dirt road
that brought us to the rear
of the Saint Mary's Cemetery.
The front gate, we knew,
was almost always locked.
We climbed over the old stonewall,
avoiding clumps of poison ivy,
and lifted our buggies over.
If the gardener were there
he'd chase us away, but no one saw
his car or heard the mowers.
Before us stretched the hill —
so much like a Soap Box Derby
course we used their rules,
marking a starting line in chalk
on its short, flat top:
No pushing off. No rocking
forward in your car to boost
your speed. Just a clean coast
down, eyes peering up from hood-level,
head tucked low to cut your wind resistance.

I got off first as Bion counted
"Ready, set ..." I knew he always
took one long, deep breath before
he hollered, "Go!" So I was ready.
But Al's car streaked by me
by mid-hill, his white wheels
gleaming. I might as well have
dragged my brakes the way he won —
by 20 feet or more, crossing
the finish line between 2 graves
with a victory whoop loud enough
to wake the dead. He jerked on

his brake before the iron gate
and I coasted around a corner
to the one tar road across
the cemetery's front, along
the Herrick Street Extension.
It was then I saw her grave,
replete with gladiolas, wreathes
of roses bound with black ribbons,
a mound of freshly cut flowers
and the newly engraved brass plaque:
Linda Towers, b. 1938, d. 1953.
The hot sun soaked me with sweat.
My throat was dry from exercise
and shouting, I sat in my wooden
buggy, feet along the plank
under the rounded hood.
And I realized, then, that she
would never see the sunlight
or perspire in the dry heat
of June; that she would never
toss her baton high and flash
her smile at multitudes applauding
at the curbside because her head
had smacked against the long, hard
quarry stones that line old
Cabot Street, even as I stood
admiring Al's car just blocks
away from where she'd fallen,
and Dr. Girsch, the town's emergency
squad doctor and, also, coroner,
pronounced her dead.

RICHIE

(For Racin' Richie Johnson who died April 1, 2006, at Thunder Mountain Speedway, Center Lisle, NY.)

They say tell your priest and lawyer
the truth, but who you really need
to trust is your mechanic. "Do
whatever it needs," I'd tell Richie
and leave the key for my car,
and more so, for my kids'. It's
one thing to confess, another
to be stranded on the roadside.
A man who can save you from
that, truly, works miracles.

Of course, I felt a kinship with him.
My dad was an auto mechanic, so
Richie felt like family. But more than that,
he loved his work, laughed it, played
with it, took the kind of pride few
ever do, to see a car pull out with
problems solved. When he raced,
Enduro cars, he'd help his
competition fix their cars and win.

Old cowboys say they'd like to go out
with their boots on. Richie, we wanted
you to live, but what a way to go —
racing toward the front on some
mountain speedway — all the folks
you helped, we who trusted you
with our cars, our lives, the ones
who loved you, rooting for you to win.

CARS

Long before Disney made the movie,
cars could talk when I was little —
metal, Diecast, my best friends
as I lay on the carpet, building
race tracks and ramps with blocks.
The station wagon would defend
itself to a sleek Mercury, "I may
look like a box, but I can haul it."

My dad would visit buddies
who owned junk yards, as likely
looking for a car to soup up
for the races, or maybe as
a sacrifice for the demolition
derby. I'd go console the Studebaker
rusting in the rear, or open a large
shed to find a 1937 Buick,
well preserved but dusty. Seated
at its wheel, I'd ask it for a ride,
my legs still not long enough
to work the clutch and pedals.

In my still-vivid memory their voices
are really there, the cars, grateful
for the push I'd give them to speed
them down my ramps, glad someone
came to visit them in their old age
and illness. Now, I wonder who
will tend my car as I grow old.

My 1968 Olds Cutlass 442 just needed TLC for it to develop some very mean intentions.

FRAME UP

The kid I bought it from didn't know
how to get it running. It was drivable
but stalled when you'd least expect it:
a 1968 Olds Cutlass 442 convertible,
in what you'd call "restorable" condition,
except someone had swapped out
the engine for a rebored 451 so
for purists, the numbers didn't match.

I got it to my friend's body shop
without a flatbed. Then, the dissection
began — piece by piece to strip it,
cure the rusted wheel wells, weakened
bumpers, and clear the interior to re-
upholster. We got it pretty close
to frame up. This was not your
granddaddy's car, kept mint in his
garage, only driven on Sundays.

A series of owners — mostly kids — had
fudged the Bondo, messed with the engine
and, most of all it turned out, screwed up
the wiring so we had to rip the harnesses
out and just replace them.

A metallic, forest-green Imron paint job
later, a new white top and new interior —
it looked as buff as that blond guy who
pumps iron at gym. And then the engine,
not just tuned to roar, but chromed
to show off in all its 4-barreled glory

when I opened the hood. But where
to test it? I got it up to about 135
one night on a deserted parkway,

mist rising from pine barrens
around me. I'm not sure it was fear
of spinning out or the size of the ticket
that made me let off the gas,
but it had lots more to go.

That was some car! Stop at a light,
race the engine, plant a left foot on
a brake and wait for the green.
Leave rubber for a half the block
with a cloud of smoke and a squeal.

I gave an old friend whiplash and he
was duly peeved! But best of all,
driving to the local 7-Eleven, I could just
sit with the top down by the front door
waiting for kids to come out of the store
and tell me, "Nice car!" I know I
looked much older than them, but
that made me feel about their age.

FORTUNATE

The autograph line was long for 4
medal of honor winners celebrated
at the Daytona 4th of July races.
Each had his story read aloud at
the opening ceremonies. Each sat
patiently to sign a booklet — free
for the asking. We live in a fortunate
land, where folks can pay small
fortunes to see races, buy corn
dogs and fried chicken, souvenirs
and beers. What God has to do
with it, some question. Others
aren't big on patriotism. Still,
the bravery of men under fire
could be celebrated. A man
firing wildly at the designated
enemy to save his friends is
the stuff of movies. But what
rote loyalty is doing at a racetrack,
like commandments at a courthouse,
could be questioned. Even
in this land of the free, such
moments of celebration should
also provoke introspection.

This 1935 Studebaker Commander sports a rumble seat. The long hood covers its straight-8 engine.

THE RESTORATION

It starts with not much more than
a sorry hulk. Somewhere there is
a gem hiding. Cars from the '30s
are solid steel, worthy of grinding
the rust off. Unbolt each fender,
detach the doors. Remove the seats.
Get ready to rumble. What you
can't fix, there's a hunt for at Carlisle
and in *Hemmings*. Lift out the straight-
8 and rebore. There are a thousand
parts to polish or rebuild. "Obsessive"
is required. "Compulsive" can't hurt
and you'd better have a big wallet.
Take a break to search for original
showroom booklets, magazine ads.
It's nice to make it look original, but
indulge in metallic paint and a good
clear-coat. "Commander:" a person
in authority. "Coupe:" an *enclosed
carriage for two passengers*.1935
Studebaker Commander 8,
convertible coupe with a rumble
seat — Best in Show.

ACCENTS

(Or, where do you park your car?)

If you were listening you already
made me as a Yankee, but that's
not accurate. I grew up just north
of Boston where my father built
stock cars for West Peabody
Speedway. Folks from where I
come from don't like New York
and hate the Yankees. Clearly,
I've never lost my accent and
I'm proud. I have even parked
my car in Harvard yard, though
when I went to college, at
the University of Massachusetts,
some folks still called it Mass
Aggie. So, when we talk NAS-
CAR, if not poetry, don't cross
your arms and take 2 steps back
'cause, "You ain't from 'round
here, are yo' boy?" Better, let's
make a deal. You teach me to
drawl and I'll do my John F.
Kennedy imitation for you:
"Ask not what NASCAR
can do for you, but what you
can do for your speedway."

BUT WILL HE DIE?

I put the hose in the tank
and suck. I'm siphoning
some gas from here to there.
Out comes this rush and I
swallow a big mouth full.
By the way, it doesn't burn.
It goes down smoother than
my grandfather's homemade
vodka. But geeze! Help!
So, I rush to the phone
and call the poison hotline.
"Oh, don't worry," says
a reassuring voice, "It won't
kill you. You'll just burp
and smell gas for a couple
days." Cue the friends' jokes.
"Don't light that cigarette?"
"Come by for the barbecue.
I'm out of charcoal starter."
Oh, and, "That ought to put
some octane in your
sex life." Not. Have you
ever sucked a gas hose?

or "only the oil companies
get to screw us."

or "when was the last time
you kissed a gas pump?"

or [you fill in the blank].

THE BODY SHOP

He keeps a can of WD40
by the bed. If it squeaks,
oil it. If it's rusty there's
the body shop, bondo
and a paint job. Just when
she's looking good again
he hits that low abutment.
There goes the front end.
Drag her in for an alignment.
Get her fixed and hope
there's still life in the old
engine. Used as they are,
you know how men
can love their cars.
Better put some sawdust
in the differential.

TO THE JUNKYARD

The love that's left —
old crankcase oil
that just won't drain.
I clean the plugs,
put on new wires.
The spark just
isn't there.

If there's an honest
body shop, tell me
where. But this
was no accident.
I went at it head-
long and now I
have to pay.

The engine races,
idles, quits. Rust
everywhere. In the end
it's the salvage heap.
There's barely a part
worth saving before
the crusher.

FOR HIS SON WHO TOTALED THE CAR AGAIN

He calls at 5:23 a.m. from Hancock, not saying
which state. "Dad, I totaled the car." Good
news, bad news. He is, after all, speaking.
"Closed my eyes a moment on a curve."

Only 2 years before, that beautiful
old Lincoln, totaled — an impact so fierce
the frame bent in a V. He also walked away
with only bruises, even partied later.

They say trouble comes in 3s. Cats have
9 lives. Men aren't friends until they've
fought over money and women. What is
the wisdom for fathers? Apples falling?

If he survives the next crash, let him not call me.
Rather, bring his bruised body home, which
I will prodigally hug, being an errant son
myself and clearly a major role model.

ALL SALES ARE FINAL

There is no lemon law that covers lovers.
You shop around, go for a test drive.
You pay your money and take what
you get. Divorce is the junk yard.
If only we could return to confront
the dealer, "The rear end is noisy
and the transmission leaks." No
way to get your money back
when you fall in love. But what
a ride, tearing out of that parking
lot with a giddy smile, that shine
that says everything is new — even
that new smell, which most agree
is carcinogenic, but who cares?
What you are buying are
new roads to travel, dreams of
immortality. Only, when the parts
fail, there is no turning back, no
bumper to bumper warranty — just
the wrecker, someone you give
your title to, and one last look
for small change under the seat.

THE AUTHOR

Dr. David B. Axelrod served as Suffolk County, Long Island's Poet Laureate, before moving to Daytona Beach, Florida. He is founder of Writers Unlimited Agency, Inc. (www.writersunlimited.org) which he directed for over thirty years, and also publisher of Writers Ink Press. His newest project is the Creative Happiness Institute, Inc., where he offers his services to the public.

He has published twenty books of poetry in addition to hundreds of essays and articles. He is the recipient of three Fulbright Awards, including his being the first official Fulbright Poet-in-Residence in the People's Republic of China. The New York Times described him as "A Treat!" He has shared the stage with such literary notables as Louis Simpson, Galway Kinnell, William Stafford, Robert Bly and Allen Ginsberg, performing at the United Nations and around the world. He has been translated into fifteen languages.

For appearances and workshops, contact:

David B. Axelrod
1104 Jacaranda Avenue, Daytona Beach, FL 32118
phone 386-492-2409,
email axelrodthepoet@yahoo.com
websites www.poetrydoctor.org and
www.creativehappiness.org